Relics

A Play for Four Women

David Campton

A SAMUEL FRENCH ACTING EDITION

SAMUEL
FRENCH
FOUNDED 1830

SAMUELFRENCH-LONDON.CO.UK
SAMUELFRENCH.COM

ISBN 978-0-573-13302-2

www.samuelfrench-london.co.uk

www.samuelfrench.com

FOR AMATEUR PRODUCTION ENQUIRIES

UNITED KINGDOM AND WORLD
EXCLUDING NORTH AMERICA

plays@SamuelFrench-London.co.uk

020 7255 4302/01

Each title is subject to availability from Samuel French,

depending upon country of performance.

CHARACTERS

WINIFRED

UNA

OLIVE

MRS PARKINSON

RELICS

A room which suggests a ground-floor bed-sitting room. It contains an anthology of bits and pieces usually spread around a house. Everything in the room is old - not antique but well-worn.

Until recently the place has been lived in, but already a thin film of dust has settled over everything.

Old clothes have been laid out on a bed.

UNA and WINIFRED come into the room. Each has the air of not being sure that she should be there. But whereas UNA is nervous and flustered, WINIFRED is almost aggressive. Each carries a bag or suitcase.

UNA	The front door shouldn't have been open.
WINIFRED	We're here before Olive. That's all we need to bother about.
UNA	We had the key.
WINIFRED	The key was given to us - officially. (She stands in the centre of the room as though taking her bearings.)
UNA	There was no point in collecting the key if the door was open.
WINIFRED	We have every right to be here. The undisputed right. (She puts down her suitcase.)
UNA	Someone has been careless. We ought to complain.
WINIFRED	I remember the old place.

UNA	If we don't complain someone may think that we have been careless.
WINIFRED	But not exactly like this. I remember a secretaire. At the time I didn't know what a secretaire was, but Aunt Dorothy explained it all to me.
UNA	Things may be missing.
WINIFRED	There used to be a secretaire against that wall.
UNA	I don't want to be blamed if it's missing.
WINIFRED	And a picture of 'Bubbles' hanging over it.
UNA	'Cherry Ripe'. I'm going to complain in self-defence.
WINIFRED	'Cherry Ripe'?
UNA	'Bubbles' is a little boy with bubbles. 'Cherry Ripe' is a little girl with cherries. She used to hang over the secretaire.
WINIFRED	No secretaire. No little girl. No cherries.
UNA	We're not responsible. We didn't leave the door open. We must complain.
WINIFRED	I remember that picture perfectly.
UNA	Who should we complain to?
WINIFRED	Only I remember 'Bubbles'.
UNA	Aunt Ada had 'Bubbles'. Over the meter cupboard. Aunt Dorothy had 'Cherry Ripe'.
WINIFRED	Over the secretaire. It was full of little drawers. They were shown to me as a treat, but I was never told what was in them. Aunt Dorothy had some secretive ways.
UNA	Aunt Ada had 'Bubbles'.
WINIFRED	If Aunt Ada had 'Bubbles' it must have gone to -
UNA	Oh! You don't think - a certain person -

WINIFRED	No.
UNA	A certain person may have –
WINIFRED	That certain person doesn't even know.
UNA	Doesn't she?
WINIFRED	For once we stole a march on Olive. She wasn't at the funeral. We were given the key.
UNA	It might have been the undertakers – forgetting to drop the catch after them. But you'd expect undertakers to know their job better than that.
WINIFRED	Can you smell – ?
UNA	(with a little shriek) Gas?
WINIFRED	The way the place used to smell, only stronger. Mothballs.
UNA	(sniffing) Jeyes Fluid.
WINIFRED	Mothballs.
UNA	(sniffing) Scrubbs Ammonia.
WINIFRED	Mothballs.
UNA	(sniffing) Fairy soap.
WINIFRED	Mothballs.
UNA	Mothballs?
WINIFRED	The place has been shut up for a fortnight. (She strides to the window.)
UNA	You're never going to open the window! We don't want the whole street to know. Word gets around so quickly.
WINIFRED	Let it.
UNA	I don't like to think of people thinking of us like that.
WINIFRED	Like what?
UNA	Rummaging.

WINIFRED	We're not rummaging.
UNA	That's the way they'll think about us. That's the way I should think. I don't want anybody to think I'm rummaging. Especially while I'm doing it. Do come away from the window, Winnie. They'll see you.
WINIFRED	They saw us come in. They know we're here. They know why we're here. And personally I don't give a damn. But if you're feeling sensitive - (She turns to the bed on which clothes have been laid out.)
UNA	I am sensitive. (Puts down her case.)
WINIFRED	Her clothes.
UNA	(looking away) I saw them.
WINIFRED	Give me a hand with them.
UNA	I couldn't touch them.
WINIFRED	Why not? She died of old age. There's nothing infectious about old age. At least if there is, we're already touched with it. We've all got it coming to us - if we live that long.
UNA	You are insensitive, Winifred.
WINIFRED	She was lucky. She had her full allowance - and som over. Threescore and ten plus.
	(She starts to sort through the clothes. UNA suddenly goes stiff with apprehension.)
UNA	(in a hoarse whisper) Winnie!
WINIFRED	(not hearing her) They're good, you know. Old fashioned, but good.
UNA	(still whispering) Winnie.
WINIFRED	(absorbed) Out of date, but not shoddy. She paid for these in her time. This label alone put fifty per cent on the price. Whenever that was.
UNA	Winnie.

WINIFRED	And she took care of them. Listen to those mothballs rattling. Made to last and she made it last.
UNA	(louder) Winnie.
WINIFRED	A pity I didn't know about this coat sooner: then I could have worn black at the funeral. This style's coming back. Even if it is a bit worn round the button-holes. Of course purple is quite acceptable at a funeral, but you can't beat black.
UNA	(tearfully) Winn-nee.
WINIFRED	Not that I'd ever buy black - not for regular wear. And funerals don't happen all that often.
UNA	(almost screaming) Winnie!!
WINIFRED	What's the matter with you?
UNA	Footsteps.
WINIFRED	You're hearing things.
UNA	You weren't listening.
WINIFRED	I've better things to do than to listen for footsteps. And you came along to give me a hand - remember?
UNA	A floorboard creaked.
WINIFRED	Who's surprised? This is old property. Creak? It's a wonder it isn't falling down.
UNA	Winifred, we are not alone in this house.
WINIFRED	Who else are you expecting?
UNA	I'm - not saying.
WINIFRED	She's not here, you know. Not Aunt Dorothy.
UNA	Don't say that. You don't know. Nobody knows.
WINIFRED	I do. This here is all that's left. And this won't be left here much longer - not after we've finished sorting through it.
UNA	I can feel a presence.

WINIFRED	You don't often see these nowadays. (She shakes a bizarre object - feather boa or old-fashioned underwear.)
UNA	(groaning) Oh.
WINIFRED	If you're feeling sick, go outside.
UNA	Sixty years she lived here. She moved in when she married. At her age she could have had a place in a home, but she wouldn't move.
WINIFRED	She did. In a Rolls Royce with flowers on top.
UNA	Can you be sure?
WINIFRED	Yes.
UNA	That creak was on the stairs.
WINIFRED	I shan't bring you again.
UNA	(with a shriek) Winnie!
	(WINIFRED drops the garments she was holding.)
WINIFRED	(with massive self-control) Don't -
UNA	Look.
WINIFRED	Do that -
UNA	But look.
WINIFRED	Again.
UNA	Of course if you won't look.
WINIFRED	Well, what is it?
	(UNA points to a suitcase just behind the door.)
UNA	That suitcase.
WINIFRED	You screamed like that because of a suitcase?
UNA	Wouldn't you?
WINIFRED	I'm trying hard not to spank you.
UNA	It's a strange suitcase.
WINIFRED	You'll see stranger things before you've done. She

was over eighty. There'll be things in this house we
won't even recognise. If you're going to scream at
every one of them, I'll put cotton-wool in my ears.

UNA

Would she have a new suitcase? She had nowhere
to go. And she wouldn't have gone there even if she
had. It isn't her suitcase, Winnie. I said there was
someone else in the house.

WINIFRED

It doesn't follow.

UNA

The front door was open. There were footsteps
upstairs. Here is a suitcase we don't recognise.
Well?

(There is a pause while WINIFRED makes up her
mind. She doesn't want to do anything but UNA is
obviously waiting for her to do something.)

WINIFRED

Well –

UNA

Well, then –

(WINIFRED strides to the door and shouts outside.
UNA retreats as far as possible from the door.)

WINIFRED

(shouting)   You can come out.

(There is no response.)

We know you're there.

(She looks at UNA but gets no support.)

(Shouting.)   You think you're clever, don't you?
But you won't get away with it.

(Silence.)

There's no reply.

UNA

If I were out there, I shouldn't reply.

WINIFRED

(crossing to her)   Any other bright ideas?

UNA

Well, if I were you, I'd look through the other
rooms.

OLIVE

(outside)   It won't do any good.

(UNA shrieks and WINIFRED lends support as her sister's knees buckle.
OLIVE appears in the doorway, and watches the sisters coolly smiling. OLIVE is about the same age as UNA, but has a wry sense of humour and a detached attitude lacking in either of the others. Secretly she considers herself to be intellectually and morally a cut above them.)

The other rooms are empty.

WINIFRED   Olive!

(She turns with as much indignation as she can muster, being encumbered with UNA.)

OLIVE   Hullo, Winnie.

WINIFRED   You half-killed Una.

UNA   The doctor warned me against shocks. 'No shocks, Mrs Waring', he said. Shocks are absolutely forbidden. A tap on the shoulder could prove fatal.

OLIVE   I'll bear that in mind.

WINIFRED   Sneaking up.

OLIVE   I came as soon as you called. You were expecting me, weren't you?

WINIFRED   You weren't at the funeral.

OLIVE   No.

WINIFRED   She was your aunt, too, you know.

OLIVE   Yes.

WINIFRED   I suppose that's your suitcase.

OLIVE   Yes.

WINIFRED   You came prepared.

OLIVE   Yes.

WINIFRED   Made yourself at home already.

OLIVE   Yes.

WINIFRED	Had a good look round, no doubt.
OLIVE	Yes.
WINIFRED	Trust you to be first.
OLIVE	Yes.
WINIFRED	Well, Una and I are here now, you notice.
OLIVE	Yes.
WINIFRED	From now on everything will be straightforward and above board - Una, would you mind carrying your own weight? (She shakes off UNA's embrace.)
UNA	I'd as soon recommend poison as a shock to a woman in your condition, he told me. 'You've nerves like piano wires', he said.
WINIFRED	We'll go through the rooms together.
OLIVE	I told you - the other rooms are empty. Except for curtains at the front - to keep up appearances.
WINIFRED	Do you expect us to believe that?
OLIVE	No.
WINIFRED	I wasn't born yesterday.
OLIVE	No.
WINIFRED	Olive Prendergast, it's over twenty years since we last met, and I don't think any better of you now than I did then.
OLIVE	No?
	(WINIFRED searches for a crushing retort, finds none, and makes for the door.)
UNA	I'll come with you.
WINIFRED	You'll stay here.
UNA	With her?
WINIFRED	She could have that suitcase packed, and be half-way to King's Cross before I'm down again. You'll keep your eyes open. And I'll tell you something else,

Olive Prendergast –

OLIVE	It's Turner, now. Mrs Edward Turner. Has been for fifteen years. Didn't we send you a piece of cake?
WINIFRED	If you want to throw dust in my eyes, you've got to get up early in the morning.
OLIVE	I did.
WINIFRED	All empty indeed!
OLIVE	Didn't you wonder what a chest of drawers was doing down here? There used to be a secretaire against that wall.
WINIFRED	With a picture of 'Bubbles' over it.
OLIVE UNA	(together) 'Cherry Ripe'.
WINIFRED	You just keep your eyes open, our Una. (She stamps out. Pause. OLIVE looks squarely at UNA, while UNA gives little sidelong glances at OLIVE. UNA sidles towards a chair.)
OLIVE	I shouldn't sit there if I were you.
UNA	What – ?
OLIVE	That chair's tied together with string. If it were to give way – the shock. We don't want another funeral, do we?
UNA	It's the heart.
OLIVE	I've always thought it must be a risk to have a heart. I'm in no danger. Try the bed. The bed's quite safe.
UNA	You laid these clothes out.
OLIVE	And you've sorted through them again.
UNA	No, it was Winnie who – (Suddenly realises what she is saying.) She had every right.
OLIVE	Of course.

UNA	The will said everything was to be shared.
OLIVE	I know.
UNA	We're the only surviving relations - you, me and Winnie.
OLIVE	That's so.
UNA	So we're quite entitled -
OLIVE	Help yourself. They're not my style.
UNA	We were given the key. We certainly didn't expect to find you.
OLIVE	You meant to be first.
UNA	Yes. I mean - you were unexpected.
OLIVE	I wasn't supposed to know.
UNA	Yes. I mean no. I mean - You always did have a nasty way of twisting one's words. I mean - you're here.
OLIVE	And just as eager to get my feet in the trough as you are.
UNA	There. You see? Really!
OLIVE	There's only one difference between us. I can take a joke.
UNA	This is not an occasion for joking. Poor Aunt Dorothy.
OLIVE	Did you carry an onion in your handkerchief at the funeral? It's the only way you'd manage to squeeze out a tear. When did you last see her? Five years ago? Ten? Fifteen? Twenty? When did you last send a letter? A Christmas card? When did you even think of her?
UNA	I thought of her - frequently.
OLIVE	Did you? What can you remember? A nose. A long, thin, cold nose, slightly red at the tip, that got in the way when she kissed you. That's all I remember.

UNA	I can remember the smell of peppermint. Winnie believes it was mothballs, but I'm sure it was peppermint.
OLIVE	I remember a nose. It isn't much to leave behind. A smell of peppermint and a nose.
UNA	She left more than that.
OLIVE	Here comes Winnie again, clattering down the stairs. No carpet on the stairs. Can Winnie take a joke?
	(WINIFRED appears, panting, in the doorway.)
WINIFRED	They're empty. All empty.
OLIVE	I did find a piece of dry soap in the bathroom.
WINIFRED	They've been stripped. Not a stick. Not a stitch.
UNA	Upstairs?
WINIFRED	Everywhere. It's desecration.
OLIVE	Not desecration, Winnie. Property isn't holy. Desirable, but not holy. And Aunt Dorothy was no saint.
WINIFRED	She had money. We know that.
OLIVE	Had. That's what we've been. Had.
WINIFRED	Property has been removed without our knowledge or consent.
UNA	We ought to complain.
WINIFRED	Well, everything's going back. I know my rights. Whatever you took from those rooms is going back.
OLIVE	Dust on my shoes. But you raised as much. Let's count our share of the dust as equal.
UNA	I think the police should be told.
OLIVE	No.
WINIFRED	Scared? What became of 'Cherry Ripe'?
OLIVE	That's a thought. Somebody actually paid good money for it.

WINIFRED	You know that much, do you?
OLIVE	Elementary. If somebody hadn't bought it the picture would still be there.
WINIFRED	You heard that, Una.
UNA	Yes, Winnie.
WINIFRED	Well, who was it?
OLIVE	Yes, indeed. Who'd want 'Cherry Ripe'? Incredible.
WINIFRED	You sold it.
OLIVE	I did?
WINIFRED	Somebody did. With all the rest. And you don't want the police called in.
OLIVE	What are the police going to see? Three vultures squabbling over dry bones. Let's keep our humiliation to ourselves.
MRS PARKINSON	(outside) Anybody there?
OLIVE	If we can.
MRS PARKINSON	(outside) Hullo?
WINIFRED	(to UNA) Did you leave the front door open?
UNA	It was open.
WINIFRED	Now we'll have half the street in.
	(MRS PARKINSON, a cheerful, imperturbable person appears in the doorway.)
MRS PARKINSON	There you are. I'd been keeping an eye open, but I was down at the shops after all. That's life, isn't it? You'll be the nieces, won't you?
WINIFRED	Mrs Beadle and Mrs Waring.
OLIVE	Mrs Turner.
MRS PARKINSON	I'm Mrs Parkinson from next door. Mrs Wilkinson said you must be the nieces when she saw you bringing the cases.

WINIFRED	We didn't hear you knock.
MRS PARKINSON	I got used to popping in to make sure she was all right. She shouldn't have been on her own at her age but she was independent. 'Time enough to be looked after when I can't look after myself,' she said.
UNA	Did she?
MRS PARKINSON	But that never happened. Went off in her sleep. A lovely way to go. I found her, you know - just popped in for a peek at her and there she was - gone.
WINIFRED	You popped in.
MRS PARKINSON	I was popping in and out all the time. A bowl of soup here. A slice of toast there. 'I've made too much for Wilfred and me,' I'd say. 'Be a love and finish it up or it'll be thrown away.' She'd take it then as a favour to me. It had to be put as a favour to me, you understand. She'd never accept a favour from anybody. She had standards.
OLIVE	Some of us do.
WINIFRED	(heavy with meaning) So you'd know where everything was.
MRS PARKINSON	I thought some little thing to remind me - 'They'll never object,' I said to Wilfred. 'What you've never had you never miss.' Some knick-knack. It's not the value, it's the sentiment. Like - er - (Her hand hovers over a small item on the shelf but it is not worth consideration. She moves on to another, and another. But not one is really worth picking up.) Or - er - I'm sure she'd have wanted - Just a - To be remembered, you see. Maybe - The fact is, there isn't anything worth taking.
OLIVE	We had noticed.
WINIFRED	(accusingly) Where did it all go?

MRS PARKINSON	Go?
WINIFRED	The musical box.
UNA	The convex mirrors.
WINIFRED	The fire-screen.
UNA	The Complete Works of Sir Walter Scott.
WINIFRED	Cherry Ripe.
OLIVE	The secretaire.
MRS PARKINSON	Now you are taking me back. I can just remember the secretaire going.
WINIFRED	Where?
MRS PARKINSON	To the auctioneers, of course. We hadn't long moved in when we noticed that being moved out. I told Wilfred to lend a hand, but it wasn't needed. The removal men knew what they were about. It was an expensive piece. She said it took up too much room and harboured dust. I could see her point of view. The valuable pieces went first.
OLIVE	To the auctioneers?
MRS PARKINSON	Then the rest, bit by bit. I suppose nobody would have what's left. Even the second-hand trade can be choosey. When we tried to part with our old three-piece do you think we could sell it? We had to pay the dustman in the end. That's life, isn't it? I did think this ornament, but - (Her hand hovers over a vase.)
OLIVE	I'm sure my cousins won't object.
	(MRS PARKINSON picks it up.)
MRS PARKINSON	(disappointed) It's been mended in two places.
WINIFRED	She - sold - everything?
MRS PARKINSON	She had to live. But it was a funny thing - as she parted with the stuff she seemed to get dimmer.
WINIFRED	Dimmer?

OLIVE	You mean absent-minded?
UNA	Vaguer?
WINIFRED	Not all there?
MRS PARKINSON	Yes. Not all there. But not the way you mean it.
WINIFRED	How do you mean it?
MRS PARKINSON	Well, you could pass her on the street and hardly notice her.
UNA	Self-effacing. I know.
WINIFRED	I don't remember her like that.
MRS PARKINSON	You didn't see her at the end. As though the real her had been tied up with the things. As her bits and pieces went away, part of her went too. Until there was nothing left. At least nothing worth holding on to. Then she went. Pouf. Like a candle flickering out. It was a shock to me to see the coffin; to think that anyone so insubstantial should still need something as solid as polished wood and brass handles.
WINIFRED	It - all - went?
MRS PARKINSON	I suggested letting rooms. 'Nobody would think the worse for letting in this day and age,' I told her. But she had those standards.
OLIVE	It still happens.
MRS PARKINSON	If she let rooms, people might think that she was in need, and she wouldn't have anybody think that. Whenever a self-denying envelope came through the door, she always put something in. A brave old soul. Even if a bit obstinate. Well - it's been a pleasure - (She goes to the door.)
WINIFRED	All - sold.
OLIVE	I wonder what a wild goose looks like.
WINIFRED	Eh?
OLIVE	We've been chasing one.

(MRS PARKINSON turns at the door.)

MRS PARKINSON   You've found the box, of course.

UNA   The box?

MRS PARKINSON   I never saw what was in it because she kept it locked. Once I came in a bit sudden like and she slammed the lid shut. Rather short she was that day. She always took great care of the box.

WINIFRED   Oh, that box. Yes, yes.

UNA   What box?

WINIFRED   The box.

MRS PARKINSON   You know about the box, then?

WINIFRED   We've got it in hand.

MRS PARKINSON   I thought I ought to mention it. I wouldn't want you to pass it over as of no account.

OLIVE   There's no danger.

MRS PARKINSON   Thank you for the - It'll remind me.   (With a glance at the vase she holds, she goes out.)

WINIFRED   Una, drop the catch on that front door.

UNA   A box?

WINIFRED   And if there's a bolt, push it home.

UNA   We haven't found a box.

WINIFRED   We're going to. And we don't want to be disturbed again, do we?

UNA   I'd better shut the front door.   (She goes out.)

WINIFRED   You can see it all now, can't you?

OLIVE   No.

WINIFRED   She had money.

OLIVE   It was said.

WINIFRED   They get like that, you know. They want it in their hands.

OLIVE	Do they?
WINIFRED	They want the money where they can count it.
OLIVE	If they've got it.
	(UNA comes back.)
UNA	There were two bolts and a chain.
WINIFRED	Banks are no good. They've got to feel it between their fingers.
UNA	Feel what?
WINIFRED	They know they can't take it with them, but they try. They keep it by them to the end. She did.
OLIVE	Did she?
UNA	What are you talking about?
WINIFRED	The box. The box Aunt Dorothy kept all her money in.
OLIVE	In theory.
WINIFRED	Can you doubt it?
OLIVE	I doubt everything till I see it.
WINIFRED	Don't you understand? That's why everything was sold - to convert it into money. That's why there's nothing in the bank. It's all in hard cash.
UNA	In a box?
WINIFRED	The old miser.
OLIVE	Poor auntie. Half a dozen words and her reputation's gone.
WINIFRED	Your fingers are twitching for your share.
OLIVE	Anybody can keep a box. I've one full of bobby-pins.
WINIFRED	You don't hide it.
OLIVE	I don't display it. Who wants to see my bobby-pins?
WINIFRED	Now where would an old lady hide a box? Look

	under the bed, Una.
UNA	I'm not sure that I like to.
WINIFRED	You'd like to lay your hands on thousands, wouldn't you?
OLIVE	Own up, Una.
WINIFRED	Then look under the bed.
UNA	Oh, well –

(Reluctantly she goes down on her hands and knees. WINIFRED goes to the chest of drawers and starts to pull out the drawers.)

WINIFRED	Didn't mean to see her cash dipped into for death duties. Convert it and hide it, that's the ticket. Why should the Government lay their thieving hands on it?
UNA	I can see something.
WINIFRED	It's there!
UNA	But it isn't a box.
WINIFRED	There might be money in it.
UNA	Not that. Not an old boot. What now?
WINIFRED	In the bed, noggin. If it isn't under the bed, it could be in the bed.
OLIVE	A bit lumpy to sleep on, don't you think?
WINIFRED	She knew what she was doing. Don't stand about, Una.

(As UNA starts to pull the bedding apart, WINIFRED turns back to the chest of drawers.)

OLIVE	Hope springs eternal.
WINIFRED	You're not doing much to help.
OLIVE	I'm enjoying myself in my own way.
WINIFRED	Underclothes. Not many either.

OLIVE	Do you think she sold the rest?
WINIFRED	This drawer's empty.
OLIVE	It might be jammed at the back.
WINIFRED	Ah-ha!
	(She pulls the drawer right out and it falls on the floor with a bang. UNA gives a shriek.)
	It isn't.
UNA	You know what shocks do to me.
OLIVE	Think twice before you find the money. Your heart might not take the strain.
UNA	It isn't in the bed. It isn't under the bed.
OLIVE	Under the carpet?
WINIFRED	There isn't a carpet.
OLIVE	Under the floorboards?
WINIFRED	You can laugh.
OLIVE	I know.
WINIFRED	It's your money as well as ours. She kept it here.
OLIVE	She kept something. Her dignity.
WINIFRED	What's dignity?
OLIVE	I lost mine for a while. I'm trying to recover it. She had standards. Will you go shares in them?
UNA	Winnie! The chest of drawers.
WINIFRED	I've been through it.
UNA	Not in. On top. With a lace doyley and a photograph on top.
WINIFRED	Ah! (She sweeps off the photograph and the lace and grabs the box.)
OLIVE	(taken aback) So there was a box.
UNA	Where anybody could see it.

WINIFRED	Cunning. Cunning. She knew the best place to hide it.
UNA	It's a pretty box.
OLIVE	Expensive.
UNA	Worth six pounds, do you think?
OLIVE	Nine, perhaps.
WINIFRED	Maybe twelve.
OLIVE	Or even fifteen.
UNA	Twenty-one?
WINIFRED	I shouldn't wonder.
OLIVE	But she kept it.
UNA	To hoard her treasure in.
WINIFRED	What better? This is the box. This. Only it's locked.
OLIVE	Let me try.
WINIFRED	Can't wait to get your hands on it now, can you?
OLIVE	There must be a key somewhere. On the mantelpiece.
WINIFRED	In a drawer.
UNA	In the bed.
	(They search for the key but without success.)
OLIVE	It isn't here.
WINIFRED	What if it was buried with her?
UNA	She's watching us. I know she is.
WINIFRED	There was a knife in one of the drawers. Just slip a knife under the lid, and push it along. I've often done it.
OLIVE	Have you?
WINIFRED	Sarcasm! (She picks up a knife and tries to

force the lock. She is aware of the growing
impatience of the others as she fails.)

UNA   You never used to be so slow getting into my
money box.

OLIVE   If you don't want me to help –

WINIFRED   It's not that sort of box. We could have a key made.

OLIVE   And who holds the box meanwhile?

WINIFRED   I'll have to take it away.

OLIVE   Will you? And who'll be present when you open up?

WINIFRED   If the box can't be opened –

OLIVE   Break it.

UNA   But it's such a pretty box. Expensive, you said.
Twenty-one pounds would be seven pounds each.
Enough to cover our expenses.

OLIVE   Is it more valuable than what's inside?   (She
picks up a poker from the hearth.)

UNA   It's a shame.

OLIVE   You don't have to watch.

(But they form a tight group as WINIFRED puts
the box on the floor, and OLIVE beats it with the
poker. UNA gives a little squeak with every blow
until the last.)

UNA   Oh. Oh. Oh. Oh. Oh. Oh. Oh. Oh. Ah!

WINIFRED   There!

(There is a long pause.)

OLIVE   Thousands?

(UNA takes a doll from the box.)

WINIFRED   It was hers.

UNA   When she was a girl. She told me so.

OLIVE   She let me hold it once. Not for long. She didn't

	trust children. They break things.
WINIFRED	The moths have been at it. (She takes a pipe from the box.)
OLIVE	Uncle Arthur's.
WINIFRED	I don't remember him.
OLIVE	Nobody does.
UNA	I was told about him. He was our uncle.

(OLIVE picks up a small box.)

OLIVE	This is pretty.
WINIFRED	But not valuable.
OLIVE	No. Not valuable. It rattles.
WINIFRED	Is it - ?
UNA	It might be.
OLIVE	Do you think it is?
WINIFRED	There's nothing else valuable.
UNA	It's a box inside a box. It ought to be precious.
OLIVE	You open it, then. I refuse to harbour any more expectations. I've lowered my standards enough for one day.

(She hands the little box to UNA, who opens it. UNA gives a shriek and drops it.)

UNA	That was a mean trick to play.
OLIVE	What was it?
UNA	You know all about my heart.

(WINIFRED goes down on her knees, then looks up.)

WINIFRED	It was a tooth.
OLIVE	A tooth?
WINIFRED	A baby tooth.
OLIVE	We had a cousin Adrian.

UNA	Adrian?
OLIVE	Before your time. He was drowned in the canal when he was six.
WINIFRED	A baby tooth.
OLIVE	Anything else?
WINIFRED	A silver bell off a wedding cake. An invitation to something. It says 'Please come to my seventh birthday party'.
OLIVE	Oh, no. That's rubbing it in too hard. (She turns brusquely away, goes to the door, and picks up her suitcase.)
WINIFRED	A birthday card. A key.
OLIVE	It won't fit anything.

(WINIFRED stands up, leaving the box on the floor.)

WINIFRED	I suppose not. Are you going?
OLIVE	You can give my share to Oxfam.
UNA	The box was the only thing worth taking.
OLIVE	We broke that.

(WINIFRED picks up her bag.)

WINIFRED	Half a minute. I'll come with you. Una?
UNA	She didn't have much at the end.
OLIVE	Only her standards. We couldn't share them, even if we wanted to.

(UNA goes out, followed by WINIFRED. OLIVE comes back and picks up the doll.)

Moths get at everything.   (She drops the doll back into the box and leaves the room.)

CURTAIN

MADE AND PRINTED IN GREAT BRITAIN BY
LATIMER TREND & COMPANY LTD PLYMOUTH
MADE IN ENGLAND

Lightning Source UK Ltd.
Milton Keynes UK
UKOW06f2344140116

266408UK00001B/90/P